# CHOICES

NANCY BYRNE

BALBOA.
PRESS

A DIVISION OF HAY HOUSE

Balboa Press books may be ordered through booksellers or by contacting:

Balboa Press
A Division of Hay House
1663 Liberty Drive
Bloomington, IN 47403
www.balboapress.com
1 (877) 407-4847

Printed in the United States of America.

ISBN: 978-1-5043-2648-3 (sc)
ISBN: 978-1-5043-2649-0 (e)

Library of Congress Control Number: 2015900402

Balboa Press rev. date: 02/02/2015

# ACKNOWLEDGEMENTS

First and foremost, I want to thank the true author of this book, Spirit, for entrusting me with the message and for believing that in spite of my many "computer challenges," I would somehow be able to get the message typed and delivered!

I would like to thank my husband, Philip Joseph Byrne IV, for his encouragement throughout this process "to stay on track and finish the book." When I had questions or doubted my abilities, he would always direct me to "Why don't you just ask the Author of the book what you're supposed to do next"! In spite of the fact that both Spirit and I teased him relentlessly throughout the book, he kept his usual good sense of humor and never doubted either of us.

I want to thank Autumn Shields for allowing me to use her picture on the cover of "our" book. The picture was symbolic of the CHOICES we all have to make from time to time; frightening and overwhelming as they may seem…when we listen to and follow our inner guidance, Spirit, we are **guaranteed** to find the happiness we seek.

In an effort to forge a better life for herself and her son, Autumn showed great courage in leaving the comfort and security of her family, friends and all of her acquaintances behind to embark on a new life in Maui which is where the photo was taken. I love you Autumn!

And last but certainly not least, I want to thank Samantha Astarte, my Doberman and best friend, pictured with me on the Author photo for coming into my life and teaching me about unconditional love. The CHOICE to let her go was one of the hardest I've ever had to make!

Oops, not done yet, I really want to thank Kari Helmer with Balboa Press for her <u>extreme</u> and unwavering patience in helping me get this book out there! I couldn't figure out how to do <u>anything</u> that was required of me (even when she sent step by step instructions; and PICTURES) and yet....with her support, it was all accomplished!

# CONTENTS

IN THE BEGINNING ............................................................................................ 1

THAT WAS THEN...THIS IS NOW! ............................................................... 6

THE SAGA CONTINUES ............................................................................... 12

MISGUIDED AND MISTREATED ............................................................... 15

TO BE OR NOT TO BE .................................................................................. 19

ONLY THE LONELY ...................................................................................... 22

YOUR PERCEPTION IS YOUR REALITY ................................................. 27

OOPS .............................................................................................................. 30

A TALE OF ZOMBIES AND THE LIVING DEAD ................................... 35

HEAVEN OR HELL... PURGATORY ....................................................... 39

ALL ALONE IN THE CROWD ..................................................................... 43

CINDERELLA, SNOWWHITE....SHRECK! ............................................ 47

WHAT THE HECK WAS THAT ABOUT? .................................................. 50

SPIRITUAL COMMUNICATION OR SELFISH BANTER ..................... 54

THE WICKED STEPMOTHER...FACT OR FICTION? ........................... 60

ATTACK OF THE KILLER GRAPE ............................................................ 63

"THE MORNING AFTER" ............................................................................ 70

FAMILY DYNAMICS ..................................................................................... 77

SISTER SANDPAPER OR, ... THE TRIPLETS ........................................ 81

CLUELESS IN NEW HAMPSHIRE ............................................................ 88

# IN THE BEGINNING

It is important to know the truths about our existence: We are not alone—we have hundreds, thousands, millions of spirit guides, angels, ascendant masters, animal guides and teachers who are looking out for our best interests every single day of our lives.

Why then, you might ask, is my life so complex, so unorganized and in so much turmoil? For one simple reason and only one: You do not yet realize that you are worthy to receive assistance from such highly recognized and important beings. Therefore, you do not ask for their assistance. And, if you ever do, it's just a matter of formality and you ask with doubt in your heart, never truly believing that you will receive anything but more bad luck. This is a deadly spiral that we all, at some time or another, bring upon ourselves.

I read somewhere that the Angels in heaven are jealous of us because we are here on earth in magnificent, earthly, bodies and have the opportunity to grow and to become all that our souls' desire for us. Yet, we slumber, we complain, we argue, we negate so many of our precious Spirit-given gifts simply because we refuse to use them. Spiritual muscle is very much the same as *physical* muscle...*you use it or you lose it!*

Too many times we allow fear of the unknown to cloud our decision making. A leap of faith seems totally out of the question but, a leap of faith is sometimes exactly what is required.

Believe and it shall be made manifest to you. Don't be like Doubting Thomas that had to see for himself with his physical eyes, and touch with his physical hands. See and touch with your spiritual eyes and your spiritual hands, for only then have you fully felt and seen.

For as the Divine is Spirit, so are you. We are in this world but not of this world. We are truly of Spirit, so why have we been hitting our physical heads against a brick wall trying to solve spiritual matters with a physical brain?

There is a verse about the definition of insanity: it's when we exhibit the same behavior as we always do (do the same thing) and expect different results. It's not working folks… isn't it time we tried a different approach?

Instead of trying to "force" things into existence how about if we just "asked" or "invited" them into our lives. What a complex, highly evolved concept huh?

Seriously, why not give it a try, as far-fetched as it may seem to you. What on earth or in the cosmos, do you have to lose?

Would your father, if asked for a piece of bread, give you a Scorpion? How rude would that be? Also, very dangerous both to you and your father! Ask and ye **SHALL** receive, it doesn't say; some of the time, none of the time or NEVER. It says; ask and you **shall** receive. I've always wondered how we, as human beings, can profess never-ending faith, and then we don't believe a word that God, "supposedly" said. That's right, I said the **S** word, supposedly – now, don't go getting self-righteous on me, you don't believe it yourself. Truthfully, do you embrace it totally? <u>IF</u> you did, you would be acting on it. You would be embracing the word of God <u>IF</u> you truly believed that God spoke those words or by divine intervention gave them to his apostles. And <u>IF</u>, you believed that you, as children of God were truly worthy of ALL the gifts and rights bestowed upon you as God's heirs to his throne, would you be dwelling in poverty, in despair, in anger, in jealously? <u>IF</u> you believed, you would be living a full, prosperous, happy life! **IF** actually has some enormous connotations, for such a small word, **IF** you really think about it.

Talk is cheap, but have you ever noticed how everyone (hypocrites that we all are at some time or another), is so nice to one another in the church setting? Why, you even tell each other how much you love them as you put on your little pious masks…and then…you try to run each other down as you race to get out of the church parking lot. After all, you are on a mission to get to the grocery store; pick up your twenty-four packs of beer and chips and prepare to watch the BIG GAME!

I believe, and I really feel I've got the Divine on my side on this issue, that faith is a way of life! It's not just going to church on Sunday for an hour or two. You live your life 24 hours a day, seven days a week, four weeks a month, and twelve months a year. Is it too much to ask to give Spirit more than just one or two hours a week every Sunday, or sometimes Saturdays, as the case may be. I think God's getting the short end of the stick in this bargain! In fact, you live, you work, you play around other God-like creatures; the birds, the bees, fish; all manner of living creatures, yes, even the trees that the granola lovers like to hug; these living things were all created by the same Supreme Spirit that breathed the breath of life into you and yet, you feel that they are inferior to you. Just something to think about.

Another little tidbit for thought is that we were **ALL** supposedly created equal! Yes, even your husband's ex-wife ladies! You know, the one you're still jealous of, even though she's no longer remotely interested in him..in fact, she thanks God every day that he's no longer in her life. (I know, I'm really going for the jugular here because the truth sometimes hurts, but please, just deal with it)! Maybe that's the point, you're jealous of her because she is so much smarter than you! She knew when to get out! Just saying!

Spirit hands out "gifts" to everyone without any qualifiers. It doesn't matter if you belong to the "only" true church; it doesn't matter if you are Catholic, Baptist, Mormon, or

Buddhist; it doesn't matter what political party you belong to, nor does the color of your skin matter. For it is only man, in his own insecurity that demands to be part of an elite group in order to raise himself above another. There's a verse that says that instead of raising the bar, we cut off other people's heads to make ourselves taller! How sad that is, it is truly pathetic…wouldn't it just be so much better to lend a helping hand to someone in need? We have all at one time or another been there ourselves…come on; admit it! I'm not talking about doing this only when you are inside of a church or sacred building. Because you know what…**YOU ARE A SACRED BUILDING**; your body houses your Spirit which is Divine and you can't hide the truth of who you are from the Divine or from yourself. Eventually, it all comes to the forefront.

# THAT WAS THEN...THIS IS NOW!

Why do we insist on living in the past, why do we project ourselves into the future? The only sure thing is **NOW**, right this moment! The next moment you could be hit by a drunk driver or worse; someone <u>from your church</u> could smack you with their Bible and break a vital blood vessel! Cherish what you have, hold it in your heart…not too tightly but in an attitude of gratitude. Be grateful for whatever it is that you have been given and, NO, you have not been given disease and/or financial ruin…that's you! You chose those lessons yourself. For whatever reason, we create our own destinies and believe it or not, there is <u>always</u> a Pay Off to our behavior or we wouldn't do it.

Hey, I'm not casting stones here. If you could've seen my life you would ask yourselves… "what the heck was she thinking?" That's the point, there's no thinking involved, your soul knows and selects the lessons it needs to grow and mature in this life prior to even being born!

Well, this certainly puts a new twist to the term "reborn" doesn't it? My ego, my physical self certainly has wished that I could have "do overs" and be reborn to a nice family; one who loved me, one who didn't beat me on a daily basis, one who didn't wish I had never been born (ouch). But alas, that was not to be.

**I AM A REMARKABLE HUMAN BEING AND I LOVE EVERYTHING ABOUT MYSELF!** No, <u>really</u>, I am who I am because of the life I've experienced! I have more integrity than anyone else I have ever met, I am extremely loyal and I am a caring and giving individual.

I have a theory, I call it <u>The Wildflower Theory</u>: Once when I was hiking in the mountains of Colorado, (I absolutely love being in Nature), I came upon a boulder in the middle of a rushing stream. Growing out of the middle of that boulder was a beautiful Daisy! Its leaves were stretched towards the sun and it was basking in all its splendor…it was magnificent. It was an eye opener to me to see this delicate looking flower surviving in such a harsh environment. That little Daisy certainly had the will not only to live but to flourish as well and certainly seemed to be enjoying its environment! Not only that but it served as a reminder to everyone who passed by and gazed upon its beauty that NOTHING is impossible if you want it to happen.

You know how you just can't get rid of those "damn" (oops, sorry) weeds that plague your garden and lawn? They seem to have an insurmountable will to survive. Then you purchase a cute little rose from the nursery that's been pampered; it's been watered regularly, fertilized and sung to on a daily basis (okay, so I'm getting a little carried away). You take the little darling home and plant it under optimal conditions and within two to five days the delicate little "wimp" dies!?!?!?

Well, I like to think that I and many others like me are Wildflowers. Having survived less than optimal childhoods, marriages or just life situations…we have decided to make the very most out of what we have been given, trust in Spirit and "know" that we can be whatever it is we want to be!

My very first memories of life on this earth were when I was about one and a half years of age. My family had gone to the Arkansas Valley Fair in Rocky Ford, Colorado. As a very small child, I remember that it was a magical experience for me; initially that is. I was intrigued by the bright lights, the festive atmosphere and all the people (well, as many people as you can have in a town the size of Rocky Ford, which is a small farming community.) I was squealing with delight and pointing at everything and everyone, so enthused was I about everything.

Then, someone mentioned to my father that I was such a cute little girl and I looked just like my "da da" and wouldn't it be so nice for my parents to let me go on a ride? I think the well intentioned individual was suggesting that they put me on a kids ride??? My dad took the bait, always seeking recognition from his peers, and before I knew it, I was strapped into this huge tub-like apparatus that spun violently around while turning on a platform that not only also was spinning but rose off the ground. You're familiar with the type of rides that now require you to be a certain height before you can get on? Yipers! That ride was a lot for a one and a half year old to handle! In fact, it was way too much!

Anyway, getting to the point here, I was terrified. I screamed, okay, screamed is a politer version of screeching, so loudly in fact, that the ride attendant stopped the ride and had my parents take me off. Bad move on my part, really bad move! My father was enraged. So much, in fact, that we immediately left the fair and went home. Upon arrival at our humble abode, my dad ordered my mother to strip me down to my diaper and proceeded to beat me to a bloody pulp!

I remember that I had no idea what I had done and had never seen my dad so upset before. Now I was really frightened but somehow, I knew I had to keep silent, no matter what! After the beating was over my father paced back and forth showering me with a barrage of profanity and expressing his hatred towards me. All the while, my mother, on her hands and knees, wiped the blood from my small body as I sat upright in a wooden, straight back chair.

Definitely, <u>no wimpy flower here!</u> What I'm trying to say is that no matter what type of life you've led or experiences you've had—you are the product of those experiences. And, the choice is yours; YOU get to decide whether your experiences end up being for the better or for the worse! If you're strong and have the will to live..GOOD FOR YOU! You can help many others who have also had less than optimal pasts. But, if on the other hand, you give up, give in to the "poor me's" and become a victim because of all your hardships than that is what you become—a victim, bounced around by fate. Life happens **TO** you, you never really live your own life. And because those are the thoughts you put out there and the energy you express, you continually call one bad experience after another into your existence!

Yes, **YOU** call bad luck into your life, because that's what you expect, it's what you think you deserve, you're always looking for it right around the next corner. And you know what? Life always gives you what you expect, what you're looking for. You're never disappointed.

Someone once told me that in order to love who you are, you cannot hate the experiences that shaped you, and I believe this to be so true. Clearly, no one is asking you to love or to cherish these circumstances, situations or trials and tribulations but at the very least, it would be wise to be more accepting or tolerant of these lessons for they taught you much about yourself; and they made you strong and wise. They helped to shape the individual you are today and obviously, since you are still here, you are at the very least, a thriver! Remember that a diamond is just a piece of coal until <u>EXTREME PRESSURE</u> is applied. Anyone can be a piece of coal but a diamond is so much more valuable - - -aren't you glad that <u>YOU</u> are a Diamond?!

In Grad school one of my professors handed out a picture of a huge bird, I think it was a Pelican, that had partially swallowed a frog. Instead of "succumbing", the frog had decided to wrap his frog hands, paws (?) (what do you call frog limbs)., around the birds neck. The expression on the birds face was priceless. The caption read: DON'T EVER GIVE UP!!!

When you give up, you've lost. Have faith in yourself. You are a magnificent spirit in a human body, but you are not your body. Your spirit chose to come to this earth for a reason, why give up and fall short of your mark? You'll just have to repeat the lesson later on and it just keeps getting harder and harder. Listen to the voice of experience here!

Believe in yourself, no matter what anyone else says. What do they know anyway. Most people, yes, parents included, criticize you because they are unhappy with their own lives.

History books are full of stories about people who in spite of having faced insurmountable odds have became famous or even became a president, like Abraham Lincoln, or, Thomas Edison who experienced so many failures before he finally succeeded and the list goes on and on. Look at the movie _**Rudy**_. This kid desperately wanted to play football for Notre Dame. He didn't have the stature or the speed, but he had the will. Some people scoffed, no one took him seriously…BIG MISTAKE!

Just like the bird in the last, next to last, the one before that, story, don't ever underestimate anyone and especially, **NEVER** underestimate yourself! **NEVER!** For you are a storehouse of untapped potential just waiting for the right time to peak! Seriously, if a little one and a half year old girl, with curly hair and a big mouth, could survive to write this book …ANYTHING IS POSSIBLE!

# THE SAGA CONTINUES

A shadow side of human behavior is that we sometimes have such good intentions and still manage to make so many mistakes!

Several years ago, I watched a spoof on an old Cowboy movie featuring Ann Margaret and Arnold Schwarzenegger. I think it was called <u>The Villain</u>. Arnold was featured in the role of Handsome Stranger (aptly named after the "handsome stranger" that had impregnated his mother). He was attired in all white (representing purity, I think) clothing, white boots, and even carried a white gun...he was really pure! He was a kind soul (really pure) whose life purpose was to help others.

This one particular scene focuses on a slightly built, feeble, and very old lady standing by the side of a muddy dirt road filled with the thundering sound of horses carrying their riders to their destinations. Observing the woman standing there all alone and looking oh so feeble, Handsome Stranger was filled with a compulsion so strong to help this feeble woman across the street that he jeopardized his own life in an attempt to keep her safe - - he was really pure! As they dodged a barrage of oncoming carriages and horses, Handsome Stranger kept reassuring the old woman that she was safe with him and that she could relax and should not worry. Although the woman appeared to be saying something, it was lost in the thunder of horses hoofs pounding on the ground.

Forward to next scene: Feeble, little old lady is being carried back across the road to the doctor's office...on a stretcher. She is covered from head to toe with bandages, badly bruised and obviously in great pain. Concerned, Handsome Stranger approaches the stretcher and inquires WHY she had decided to "re-cross" the muddy dirt road after he had already, gallantly, by the way, provided safe passage for her the first time. The woman's response was priceless…and funnier than heck! Enraged, she begins pounding on him, all the while showering him with abusive language (I didn't think little, feeble, old ladies knew those kind of words). This seemingly feeble old woman was intent on letting Handsome Stranger know that she had never wanted to cross the street in the first place and that he should've minded his own F_ _ _ _ n business! I tell you, this was the little, old, feeble, lady from hell! I FINALLY FOUND MY ROLE MODEL!!!!

Unfortunately, we all too frequently behave in a similar fashion as Handsome Stranger. In our eagerness to please, to provide or to be helpful, we sometimes "give" of ourselves, often to our own detriment, to others who not only are not seeking our well intentioned help, they flat out don't want it and they also bitterly resent the fact that we seem to exalt ourselves to a position of knowing more than they do, what is best for them. No one enjoys being made out to be an inferior human being who doesn't even know what is best for them…no wonder little, old, feeble, psycho lady was pissed!

Upon discovering that our gestures of kindness have not been welcomed with open arms, we are confused, we feel deflated, hurt, and often rejected. Yet, in a futile attempt to build our own self-worth, we repeatedly attempt to make ourselves useful, needed and wanted in some way, only to be slighted or downright rejected again.

# MISGUIDED AND MISTREATED

As a child who grew up in an abusive (I am the Queen of understatement here) environment, I quickly became a little helper, whose sole purpose was to provide pleasure to others. At a very young age, I washed the dishes, cooked meals and cleaned the house while my younger, prettier sister, entertained the family by telling jokes and simply being beautiful! In my desperation for attention, I guess validation is the correct word here, I protected my sister, my brother and my mother against my father's wrath, when in reality, someone should have been protecting me!

In fact, on one specific occasion that I remember, my father was pacing back and forth (I guess he was a pacer) while my mom was hand washing dishes. Each and every time he passed by her he would punch her in the head while uttering the most horrible, terrible words to her. The really sad thing about it was that my mother just kept washing the dishes, like she wasn't even human and didn't even realize what was happening. Finally, I guess Dad got tired of pacing, or perhaps he was just running out of energy, so he stopped pacing and then just proceeded, quite naturally, to the next step which was to choke my mother. As I observed this surreal drama, while sitting at our kitchen table, I noticed that my mom was actually turning purple and even at six or seven years of age; I knew this couldn't be a good sign. The frightening thought just seemed to float past my mind that my father intended to kill my mother! It seemed quite natural that I then noticed a small steak knife sitting on the kitchen table, right in front of me. As I observed the steak knife, the thought entered my mind, "I can't kill my own father"! But then, as if in a dreamlike state, I proceeded to pick up the steak knife and drive it into his ass! I still don't understand exactly what happened that day, perhaps I was disassociative, terrified for my mother's safety, or maybe, I was just a kid who liked to play with sharp objects.

At any rate, as the knife penetrated my dad's buttocks, mom fell to the floor in a heap and she looked just like a limp rag doll. Holly Moley; then, the reality of my actions finally struck home; my enraged father turned on me, his face blazing red and spittle spewing forth from his mouth. I thought I saw smoke coming from his nostrils too! He yelled at me that he was going to kill me and I believed him – go figure! He then dropkicked me from the kitchen into the living room. Even though I was six or seven at the time we barely had enough food to survive on as dad spent his money on booze and women, so I was extremely emaciated. Dad worked at the Pueblo Army Depot and wore steel tipped boots too which didn't do much to help my predicament either. When I hit the living room wall, I swear I saw my head rolling along the floor.

While this monster was walking towards me, my mother who was probably dazed and incoherent but who I was seriously counting on to save my butt; the one whose life I had just saved; got up off the kitchen floor, walked into the bedroom and shut the door. Never once did she intervene on my behalf, hell, she didn't even glance towards me. The little "protector" was on her own. I disassociated and thankfully, never felt a thing. I woke up the next morning still lying on the living room floor.

Sadly, but reasonably, as an adult, I grew up to be a people pleaser. I acquiesced, taking a back seat to everyone, thinking that everyone's needs were more important than my own. My rationale was that I was strong and that I had already been to Hell and back. I felt that others who had not suffered as much as I had were not as strong and therefore, not as capable of handling the fierce winds of adversity as I was. I repeatedly told myself "You have nothing to complain about, after all, you haven't had to hang on a cross yet!"

Yipes! This scenario is starting to sound a lot like Handsome Stranger in that movie. While no one, not a single soul, ever asked me to suffer for them, to protect them, to give up my life; my goals (what goals…I was just trying to survive), my happiness, here I was racing around like a crazy kid trying to make everyone happy! I just wanted everyone to be **h a p p y**! What the heck, since I wasn't, _someone_ should be happy!

An amazing Master, Esoteric, Numerologist, Elizabeth Summers, (elizabeth@elizabeth summers.com,) a woman I feel a deep soul connection to even though we have as yet, never met, hit the nail right on the head when she once told me that I busily psychologize and make pancakes for everyone else but that I don't seem to notice my own pain or the fact that I am starving to death. Although she is extremely accurate, I doubt that even she knew the far reaching implications of what she had said at that time. She's fantastic… check her out!

# TO BE OR NOT TO BE

While I strongly believe that we are not living in this beautiful, earthly, realm merely to meet our own, selfish needs, I do believe that we are here to LIVE! I think we are here to enjoy, yes, actually enjoy the earth, to revel in its beauty, to enjoy the pleasures of being human, to bask in the warmth of a loved one, and to be absolutely exhilarated when your grandchildren love you and deem you worthy enough to want to spend time with you on a regular basis. My grandkids don't seem to have any agendas; they just enjoy "hanging" with me! **YAY! I AM SOOOO BLESSED!**

Taking care of yourselves and your needs, your dreams and desires is essential for your survival. In psychology, we call it Enlightened Selfishness. When you are flying somewhere (I'm referring to actually flying…you know; like in an airplane!) anywhere, the Flight Attendants tell you to put the oxygen mask on yourself first. If you try to help your small child first, or your fragile mother and you become unconscious, you will absolutely not only not be in a position to help anyone else but you will not be able to help even yourself!!! Furthermore, if you become disabled, you are going to infringe on someone else's time to assist you. So you see,(self-centered person that you are, because in all actuality), you are really being quite selfish by not taking care of your own needs FIRST! Sometimes, by always being there for others; your kids, your husband/wife, your friends, your colleagues, the list can go on and on; you are actually providing a disservice to them. You could even be enabling them and thus preventing them from learning their own lessons and reaching their own fulfillment.

I remember much to my surprise, when working at an Adolescent Psychiatric Treatment Hospital; in an effort to comfort a young rape victim, a seasoned therapist put his arm around her and she literally "lost it"! We sometimes, offer comfort to others not because they need it, but because it makes us feel good. Like we're providing for a need (there we go again, needing to be useful). We like to feel that we can provide for the needs of others while all the while we are seemingly incapable of taking care of our own needs. When someone has been violated by the human touch, it's not wise to try to provide comfort by touching them! Usually, they're just not receptive to touchy feely contact at the time! Go figure! Yet, that is what we seem to want to "give them"; it's what <u>we</u> want and we haven't figured out that perhaps we could ask them…."What do YOU want me to do for you"?

# ONLY THE LONELY

We are social animals, we want acceptance, and we want to fit in with the tribe. We want so badly to be important to "someone". The problem is that we, ourselves, do not believe we are important, we don't feel accepted. In reality, we feel isolated and alone. In order to fill this need, we often seek comfort from others, but the cold, hard fact, is that no one else can make you happy. Only you can make yourself happy. You have to go within-- YES, within. You will never find fulfillment by looking for it externally. No! No guru, no therapist, no spiritual practitioner can ever give you peace or fulfillment. Only you have all the information about yourself, therefore, only **You** have the answers and the ability to change your own lives. This last part is vital so I'm going to repeat it: <u>**only you have the ability to change your own lives!**</u>

Yes, others can offer suggestions and guidance, they may genuinely want to help but no one else can do it for you. Advice is cheap (counseling is not!) If I tell you what to do and I'm wrong, and if you follow my advice, who suffers the consequences? Certainly not me. You and you alone suffer the consequences of your own actions. Conversely, you and you alone reap the benefits of your own actions - - unless, of course, you wanted to offer me a huge tip! What I'm trying to say is that it is so much better for you to take responsibility for your life rather than putting your faith, your health, your future, or you life into the hands of someone else who doesn't even have all the information they would need about you to make an informed decision.

Three years ago, I went in for my yearly check up (physical, not mental) and my long time physician found blood in my stool. She scheduled me to have a colonoscopy which revealed no problems. However, because I have a history of stomach cancer in the family it was recommended that I see a gastroenterologist and have him go in from the other direction. To make a long story short (this is a first for me), they discovered that I had acid reflex. This was the beginning of an absolute nightmare for me. I was promptly put on Acid Blockers which, of course, didn't help, so my doctor told me to take two or three a day and if that didn't work, they would perform a surgical procedure which prevents the acid from coming up. Because I had not taken responsibility for my own health, had not done any research on my own and blindly committed my health into the hands of another "more qualified" individual, my immune system all but shut down. I have since discovered that after the age of forty, your body's production of acid is reduced by 50%. You need acid to digest the food you eat! So, with no acid in my stomach to aid in digestion and help me assimilate the foods I ate, I developed immune problems, kidney infections, eye infections, skin infections, urinary tract infections, and allergies too numerous to mention.

This true saga is certainly not meant to frighten anyone or as an endorsement to boycott physicians, who do serve a purpose, i.e., if I were bleeding to death from a car accident, I would want stitches, rather than supplements. Rather, it was provided as a personal example of the devastation that can occur when you entrust your life wholly to someone else! No one else has the investment in your health that you do! Your life is the most precious gift that has been given to you. Cherish it, **LIVE IT!**

Do not turn it over to someone else who will most likely use it for their own purposes. They can play havoc with their own lives if they so choose but do not allow them to destroy yours!

I just can't emphasize this enough - - YOU ARE NOT A VICTIM! So please don't behave like one! One of my favorite quotes (I have two but I'll save the other one until the end of the book) comes from Marianne Williamson, the author of **_A Return to Love_** and was used in the Inaugural Speech of Nelson Mandela in 1994. What insight!

"Our deepest fear is not that we are inadequate..

Our deepest fear is that we are powerful beyond measure.

It is our light, not our darkness that most frightens us.

We ask ourselves, "Who am I to be brilliant, gorgeous, talented & fabulous?"

Actually, who are you not to be?

You are a child of God.

Your playing small doesn't serve the world.

There's nothing enlightened about shrinking so that other people won't feel insecure around you. We are all meant to shine, as children do.

We are born to make manifest the glory of God that is within us.

It's not just in some of us; it's in everyone.

And as we let our own light shine,

We unconsciously give other people permission to do the same.

As we're liberated from our own fear, our presence automatically liberates others."

The birds instinctively know when to fly south for the winter. The trees instinctively know when to turn their leaves upward to catch the moisture during a rainstorm. In the physical realm, Police Officers are equipped with guns, knives, mace and clubs. It would be ludicrous to send them out without the proper tools to protect themselves. Airline pilots are trained to fly airplanes and provided with all the equipment they require to get the task done. Similarly, you are also equipped with all the tools you need to live a happy, safe, successful and prosperous life. <u>You just have to be willing to use the tools you have been given!</u>

I received a book of Medicine Cards –<u>*The Discovery of Power: Through the Ways of Animals*</u> by Jamie Sams & David Carson as a gift. The Rabbit caught my attention as he is the Fear Caller. The rabbit shouts to the Eagle, "I am so afraid of you." If Eagle doesn't hear him, Rabbit calls louder, "Eagle, stay away from me!" Eagle, now hearing Rabbit, comes and eats him. Some people are like this. They are so afraid of tragedy, illness, disaster, and "being taken," that they call those very fears to them to teach them lessons. What you resist will persist! What you fear most is what you will become. Stop talking about horrible things happening and get rid of "what if" in your vocabulary. Stop now!

Sounds crazy doesn't it, yet this is exactly what we do. When we focus our energy on any thought, we actually call it to ourselves.

I once heard that Mother Teresa had turned down an invitation to attend an anti-war rally. Her rationale was that she did not want to put her energy, thoughts or intentions towards "anti-war" anything. The story goes, that she then stated that if invited, she would be happy to attend a peace rally because she supported the concept of peace. She apparently understood that whatever you put your attention and energy towards, gets drawn back to you!

# Your Perception is Your Reality

We really need to fully appreciate the fact that most of what we do and have is a result of how we think and of our own values. Do you value yourself? Do you honor yourself? Do you care for your body? Do you set boundaries to prevent others from devaluing you?

As a kid, you remember the little curly haired girl with the loud mouth, I so wanted to be "spiritual", I wanted to walk with God. In fact, I wanted very much to be just like God. Most of us however, seem to have the mistaken idea that being Spiritual or Godlike means living a life of fasting and prayer, neglecting our bodies and putting our ego's and our bodies under submission. We feel that to experience pleasure is to risk eternal damnation. That is so not the case.

If it weren't for these depraved, pathetic, sinful bodies (tongue in cheek) that house our souls, our souls would not be able to do the work that they were called to do. When the body dies, the soul leaves. Most people don't even listen fully to one another and certainly no one is going to give their full attention to a disembodied soul who's trying to provide them with direction… well, most people wouldn't that is. A disembodied soul can't build a temple, or start a charity for orphans or even wipe the tear from a child's face but a human body can accomplish __all__ of these feats!

We need to love our physical bodies, yes, and all their defects, care for them, and enjoy them. Just think about what an amazing creation your body is. It is resilient and finely tuned, more so than any motor. Your body maintains a state of homeostasis, it rejuvenates and heals itself, it adapts to environmental changes and yes, it also gives you signs and tries (futilely most of the time) to let you know when it's requirements for basic survival are not being met.

# OOPS

Because the relationship between soul and body is one of reciprocity, our souls use our body to get our attention on occasion (or in my case…..many, many, many gazillions of occasions). The stronger your soul, the stronger the message you are given. We commonly refer to this as a Wake Up Call! And these Wake Up Calls, while for your own benefit and good, can be so distracting, limiting and painful, that it is just so much better to listen and pay attention to what your soul is trying to tell you in the first place!

Usually, if we refuse to give up our Zombie state or the Living Dead State as I used to refer to myself, the soul will use finances or health to get your attention. So, while I certainly don't expect anyone to welcome financial stress, or illness with open arms, at least you might want to consider looking within to see why these circumstances are occurring seemingly **TO** you.

As always you have a choice here – you can try to ignore it (however, I can assure you it will not go away until you pay attention, being the personal "expert" on this issue, that I am!) or, the alternative is that you start paying attention to your life, and question why you do the things you do. What are your values, are you really living your life or are you just going through the motions?

Have you ever known someone who is a "Drama Queen/King"? Someone who blows everything up into a major crisis? Their symptoms are always much worse than anyone else's. Their husband/wife is a bigger jerk than all of their friends' husbands/wives put together. They have it so hard, their lives are far worse than anything Job of Bible fame, could have endured and it goes on and on and on and....on, just like a bad soap opera.

Finally, sometime down the road, people in general, even family and friends, tire of this individual. It's kind of like the story of the Boy Who Cried Wolf. Not trying to be confrontational or hurt this individual's feelings…everyone just withdraws! No one wants to be around someone who is an emotional wreck, whose life centers around personal catastrophe and someone who brings you down all the time. Their energy actually drains others…you've heard of emotional vampires? Well, guess what…here s/he is in the flesh. Oh my gosh, then when others start to avoid this person and don't want to be around them, these people feel rejected. They really don't have a clue what's going on…they believe that they are the most giving, most thoughtful (yeah, of themselves) person in the universe. They feel that just when they need a friend the most…which is actually unbeknownst to them, all of the time, everyone deserts them. It is just one more example of how bad their life is. Another term for this type of situation is self-fulfilling prophecy.

I had to do a presentation on self-fulfilling prophesy in my second year as a psychology major … (and, no, I didn't learn any lessons from my project at that time…it took many, many, many – okay, you don't need to know how very many years of experiencing this phenomena myself it took to finally wake up to what I was doing to myself!)

I came across a comic strip in the newspaper that caught my attention and served as an excellent example of self-fulfilling prophecy. It was about a young girl who was getting ready to start school and who was dreading every single minute of it because she just knew that no one was going to like her. She gets onto the bus and frowns at all the other kids as she takes a seat in the very back of the bus, far away from all the other children.

Upon arriving at school, she proceeds to scowl at all the other kids as they laughingly interact with one another. She sullenly attends classes and is firmly convinced that all the teachers are going to hate her. Then, at lunch, she is pictured sitting all alone at a very large table while all the other kids are avoiding her like the plague. She looks up, still scowling, by the way, and says to herself: "See, I knew no one would like me!"

As a comic strip it was funny and it served my purpose for the presentation. It's not so funny when we are experiencing this phenomenon ourselves. And, what makes this experience even more disheartening is that while we are going through it, we have no clue that we are creating this experience for ourselves.

It has been said that our flaws shine like neon lights to everyone who knows us, yet, we remain unaware of these defects in our character until the time for growth is ripe. I've often likened this to the story of the Emperor who wore no clothes but didn't have a clue even though his entire kingdom knew he was naked. (Oh how embarrassing!)

I have a friend who I believe, is one of the most remarkable human beings I know. This man is extremely intelligent, personable, funny, attractive and is a decent, kind, human being. Yet, others seem to view him with disdain and contempt. This person is a generous human being yet, people repeatedly take advantage of him. It is as though he has the word "SUCKER" tattooed on his forehead. He has lend his law books to other colleagues who not only have refused to return them, but when he has had need of them himself and asked to "borrow" one or two back, the individual who is using them has refused, stating that they are still using that particular book right now.

While this individual has everything personality wise that he needs to be successful and achieve prominence…he repeatedly berates himself to others. I have been to lunch with him when he has told the story to other people in the group of how his bank has mismanaged his funds and yet, he continues to bank with them; he has told the story of the law books and embarrassingly explained that he had to purchase an entire set of new law books; of how a neighbor borrowed something of his for a day and then decided to keep it. He does this continuously and even when I (ok, I'm a **close** friend…and sometimes, a meddler) have pointed this behavior out to him and he has agreed that he knows he does it, he continues to exhibit this type of behavior...ARG!

This individual is announcing to the world that he is a victim, prime for taking advantage of...he is extending an invitation for people to use him, yet, sadly, he is so disappointed each and every time someone does!

Our behavior expresses our beliefs, feelings and values. That's why the experts advise us, when given a choice between the verbal and the non verbal to <u>always</u> believe the non verbal or behavioral. People can lie (yes, it's true) but your body can't, unless of course, you're a really good, professional liar and you've trained your body to be deceptive but even then, your body prefers to tell the truth!

So you see, if you're disliked at work, at school, in your neighborhood or, if you just continuously attract the same type of person into your life, you need to look at yourself and determine what non verbal and sometimes even verbal, messages you are giving to others. Are you like the rabbit that calls out "I am afraid of you?" If so, then predators will (guaranteed) come into your life.

# A TALE OF ZOMBIES AND THE LIVING DEAD

Research shows that serial killers and serial rapists always observe, sometimes stalking their victims for days in the selection process prior to making a decision as to which person to target. They never go for the individual who appears to be confident or appears to be aware of their surroundings, or that they think will make a lot of noise and call attention to them, as predator. No, they go after the individual who seems to be oblivious or unaware of their surroundings; looking down at the ground, and malleable, someone who will follow "orders".

As previously stated, whether you realize it or not, your body gives off signals and messages to others on a regular basis. You know that verse, you know the one…from someplace, that states "if you want to have friends, you must first show yourself to be friendly? It could also say, if you want financial prosperity, you must first show yourself to be open to financial prosperity.

If you have been taught that money is the root of all evil or that rich people are dishonest and unhappy, you're probably not going to get rich because on an unconscious level, you believe that money is bad. Normal people do not knowingly bring bad things into their lives, correct? Actually, we all at one time or another do bring bad things into our lives but we are unaware of what we are doing…because we are not trusting our instincts, our signals from the Divine Spirit to guide us.

To get back to the Wake Up Call, Michael Tamura in his book <u>You Are the One</u>, describes the Zombie stage much like the sensation of having your foot fall asleep. When your foot is asleep, it is numb. You feel nothing but when it wakes up – it's quite another matter. It hurts and you don't like it

That's part of the reason we have so much trouble with addictions. We want to be numb because it prevents us from dealing with the pain in our lives. Unfortunately, as the saying goes: the only way out of the fire is through the fire! The pain of remembering memories that we have tried for so long to bury doesn't last forever and life upon awakening is so much richer, fuller and more productive than being in a zombie state. It takes courage to face reality, to look within yourselves but I guarantee, it is so much better than continuing your life as "part of the living dead", who feel no joy, experience no pleasure, or derive any satisfaction from their accomplishments. They are on automatic pilot and that's not the way to fully live a life!

Sadly, at some point in our lives we all make a bad decision, whether out of ignorance, good intentions (like Handsome Stranger) or because we have deluded ourselves; that causes another emotional pain. Tragically, some of us (you) have made very bad decisions that cause another individual great emotional pain. Most of the time even if you are really, truly sorry (after the fact) you will not be given another chance to rectify your behavior. No matter how hard you try. This may seem harsh or unjust to you, after all, you are really sorry, you apologized and everything, all to no avail.

Before you build resentment and start to dehumanize another for not allowing you back into their lives consider this: In the physical world, if you rip open someone's heart with your bare hands, you not only <u>don't</u> get to see or be with that individual again – you're probably going to be spending quite a bit of time in jail, if not in prison. You lose not only your freedom but also your rights when you are incarcerated because it is wrong (inhumane) to cause physical harm to another even if you do apologize later, providing that individual is still alive and you are given the opportunity.

A professor of mine once used the analogy of a broken window by explaining that if you break someone else's window, even though you regret your actions and apologize profusely – someone still has to pay for that window and, it's usually the individual who broke said window in the first place, providing, of course, law enforcement can find that individual.

I believe that most of the time verbal and emotional abuse is far more devastating than physical abuse. Doctors can mend broken bones (hopefully without severing an artery) and can stitch up open wounds (hopefully without severing an artery)! Emotional scars last FOREVER in most cases and always carry with them the impact of betrayal. This, by the way, is a good scenario...sometimes, the patient dies emotionally and being alive while being dead is so much worse than just physically dying!

So, if you are fortunate enough to have someone in your life that truly loves you, treat them with honor, cherish them for you are a lucky individual indeed! Do not for any reason; any momentary gain or pleasure destroy that relationship by betrayal, infidelity, rejection, humiliation, detachment or any other form of verbal or emotional abuse. For, it is truly as though someone has entrusted you with their heart and you have chosen to rip it open with your bare hands, throw it onto the ground, stomp on it and then pour salt directly into their bleeding wounds. You won't often get another chance. If, you care at all – think twice before hurting the one person you love and who loves you. I am not over exaggerating here – not at all – this is <u>exactly</u> what it feels like to the recipient of verbal and emotional abuse!

**IF**, you are fortunate enough to be given another shot at being a decent human being, DON'T SCREW IT UP! <u>N E V E R</u>, <u>NEVER</u>, <u>NEVER</u> ever again! Nu uh – NEVER!

# HEAVEN OR HELL...
# PURGATORY

Not only do we, on an unconscious basis try to provide help and assistance to others (less fortunate than we are, of course) so that we can avoid looking at ourselves and our deeper issues, (yes, it's true – that's why so many of us with childhood problems go into psychology) we often unintentionally, of course, misguide or misdirect others in order to validate decisions we have made.

While this may sound insane, it's true. Why do most of your friends try, ever so gently to get you to try out the church of <u>their</u> choice, the cosmetics they use (unless they're selling them. ...duh!), the therapist that has really helped them...<u>for thirty five years now!</u> If someone doesn't truly believe that what they are doing is right, they will enlist others to do the same darn thing because it validates what they are doing! People who have a deep seated conviction that they are doing the right thing do not have to receive the approval of others nor do they have to enlist others to follow the same course.

For example, if you don't really believe in all the teachings of your church or you doubt the validity of some cult you're in, you will then proceed to try to get as many other people as you know to become members of your church or your cult. There is power in numbers… if others you respect or admire subscribe to the same religion or belief system that you do, it not only validates and strengthens your beliefs but it makes you "right" in your own mind. Let's face it, everyone wants to be "right".

Research shows (I don't know what research...I learned this in school...so it must be "right", right?) that if someone purchases a car and it turns out to be a lemon and gives them nothing but trouble they will....are you ready for this? They will recommend that very car to their colleagues, neighbors and yes, sometimes even family. Why, on earth would anyone in their right mind provide such a disservice to others? Wouldn't it seem logical that they would advise others <u>against</u> purchasing said vehicle? Not to their subconscious egos it wouldn't...it makes perfect sense to their egos. In order to save face (with whom I do not know) with their egos presumably, and in order to avoid acknowledging the fact that they made a very costly mistake (probably against the advice of their all knowing mother...and being a mother; I personally can attest to the <u>FACT</u> that we are ALL..."ALL KNOWING"...("smile")

To the subconscious mind, the more people who purchase the same car and make the same mistake, and the more people who also were an "easy mark", the more justification the ego can get from making the mistake. Since "Everyone else made the same mistake," you can now more easily justify that you made the mistake. Not to "bad talk" the ego here, it is here to protect us and protect us it does, even if we destroy our lives in the process!

Ever notice how an individual trying to convince others of, whatever they are trying to convince others about, will "name drop" in order to create a sense of affiliation to their product, values, or beliefs or even to themselves..."even my friend who is a scientist knows etc., etc." They associate with me, so I must have their stamp of approval as a worthy human being. How sad, that we don't recognize that we are ENOUGH. We don't need anyone else to validate us, we are all EQUAL, no one is better than anyone else. If we believe in something, then we believe in it and that should be enough for us. And...if somebody else doesn't believe in it, so what, maybe it's not right for them at the time, perhaps they are on a different path. It's all good!

At other times the need for approval or acceptance is so strong that it takes the form of *gossip*, yes...*gossip!* An individual will run around telling everyone they know about this "secret" or inside information they received from someone "in the know". The implication here is that someone "in the know", had enough confidence in them to share this information with them. This just blows the credibility of someone "in the knows" reputation all to heck...what were they thinking, confiding to a gossip in the first place?! Did they want the information leaked? Is this a covert operation? Are they spies?

The fact that this secret or inside information was given to said "gossipy" individual in confidence and that disclosing this information thereby broke any bonds of trust that initially existed between said "gossipy" individual and "misguided" trusting individual says a lot, volumes in fact, about Mr/s gossip here! In an effort to get others to know how important and trusted they were, they totally betrayed the trust of another.

On some level; deep, buried, level, people know that if someone will gossip or "share" the secrets of someone else, this same individual, if given the opportunity, will do the very same thing to them. So don't give the "gossip" the same opportunity!

Important to remember: What an individual does to someone else, they will eventually do to you if given the opportunity. This is really important stuff to know.

So...therefore, if someone you are dating cheated on their spouse or a "significant other" by dating you- - Guess what? Yup! They will eventually cheat on you too when someone more desirable comes along...even it takes 15 years! This is practically a guarantee (although I've heard that Twin Flames may be an exception). If they have cheating in their blood, there is always going to be someone more desirable right around the corner.

And, don't think you get off scott free on this either: Shame on you for going after someone who has made a commitment, or entered into a contract with someone else. You reap what you sow and that's just the way it is! If you plant weeds, you are not going to reap Daisies.

# ALL ALONE IN THE CROWD

Relationships are one of the most intriguing topics today. A man, upon arriving in the United States from a foreign country commented on a radio program that in America our songs all seem to be about love. He said that in his country the songs are all about water. He then went on to state that people, in general, always write or sing about what they are lacking. WOW!

In this day and age of modern technology; with all our smart phones (I love my smart phone) computers (not so much), i pads (I love my i pad), etc., etc., we are lonelier than at any other time in history.

Go to any restaurant and observe a family enjoying a "family night out" – each family member, yes, even mom and dad, is texting someone else. There is no conversation, no eye contact, no human closeness of any kind. Even if everyone is not texting...no one is talking, they stare blankly at the wall, the table or look around the room as if desperately searching for their best friend!

Look at a group of kids walking down the sidewalk together – again, each one is texting someone else.

Several years ago, I flew into Houston to spend quality time with a girlfriend of mine. She graciously picked me up from the airport which I really appreciated, being directionally challenged...I have many challenges, this being one of the biggies!

The moment we got into her car, she called another friend. The conversation which consisted about how much fun they had had the night before, lasted halfway through the drive home. Fortunately for me, there was a break in the conversation because I desperately had to stop to pee.

Upon returning to the car after my "potty break", I found that my friend was again on the phone, this time with a suitor. I felt like a voyeur listening to the conversation…however, that didn't stop me, not at all! While I have to admit that I was extremely entertained by the part of the conversation I was privy to, I was silently praying that she would accidently put her phone onto "speaker" so that I could listen to both sides of the interaction.

When we arrived at her home, I sat on her couch for over fifteen minutes, wondering where I should put my suitcases, where I was going to sleep —and where in the heck her restroom was while she continued her animated cell phone conversation.

Once I was unpacked and thinking, erroneously, that we were finally going to have some time to "catch up" with one another, she announced that we were meeting friends for appetizers and drinks. FINE! I had only spent a small fortune on air fare and travelled several hundred miles to go to see her!

Imagine my surprise when the two friends we met turned out to be two twenty four year old males. They were younger than my oldest son! I have to admit "my date" and I had a great and deeply moving conversation about his grandma who had recently passed when I admired a bracelet he was wearing that she had made for him.

It's ironic but I didn't feel slighted at my friends behavior because she texted two of her other friends while trying to make time with her young suitor who was also texting someone else. Sadly, I didn't have a texting option at the time or E.T. would have texted home for a return flight!

The point is that we have seemingly lost our ability to connect or interact with others. We do not know how to communicate! My sons (yes, my very own sons) drive me crazy! I would dearly love to hear their angelic voices but instead I get texts. They text me when they're driving home from work and have time to "talk"?

Please, don't misunderstand, I will take whatever time I can have with them but I do worry about them texting and driving – Sigh!

# CINDERELLA, SNOWWHITE....SHRECK!

You meet someone, your heart melts, you long to be together – FOREVER! They are perfect for you. You can't live without them. *They have a cute butt!*

Fast forward two years. They are impossible to get along with. They don't do anything right. Did they forget how to brush their teeth? What happened to that cute butt?

We are attracted to someone because of their personality traits. Okay, the cute butt didn't hurt either. This individual met our needs and we liked everything (almost…it's not like we're in a deep trance here) about them and then…as if a cloud of doom descends upon us – we suddenly dislike everything about them and promptly engage in a mission to "change them", too late!

If, you're going to try to change someone and really, you can't because you can only change yourself - - but, if you could, the time would be b e f o r e you get married or move in together. But no, you were too busy admiring the cute butt to plan ahead. Once you're married, the deal is sealed. They've already got you and who wants to dissolve a marriage after two short years (a person who is self confident, loves themselves and doesn't give a damn what others think, that's who! After all, it is your life). What would your parents think? Forget the parents…your friends will all think you are a loser!

It really isn't about the situation that we are in as much as how we choose to handle the situation. While you can't change another human being, neither can they change you, unless you willingly cooperate - - DON'T DO IT! You do not have to give up your life for someone else, married or not.

I used to tell my sons – this was when they still listened to me…it was a very, very, long time ago, that any relationship involves some compromise but the one thing you can never compromise is your "essence" and I firmly believe in that to this day –cute butt or not!

Alas, it has been said that the only opportunities we have for soul growth are through relationships. Ever notice how easy it is to be calm and serene when someone else is not pointing out your flaws, putting ridiculous demands on your time or doing stupid things that you don't think they should be doing?

Life lived as a Monk in seclusion certainly has its benefits – but the only way you're going to learn about yourself and about how to get along with others is through relationships. No one promised self awareness was going to be easy!

Others reflect who you are! I know. I know, it's going to be okay. My husband and I are like "two peas in a pod", we are both Aquarians…humanitarians, not so good at one on one relationships, stubborn and we are both always right! We both have type O blood and are ENTP's in the Meyers Briggs Personality tests. Yet, we are as different as night and day – I'm Day, he's Night!

HE is the most stubborn, hard to get along with, maddening individual I have EVER met! I, on the other hand, am compassionate, selfless, willing to admit my flaws, loyal… let's just cut to the chase here…I AM A SAINT! At any rate, I am an old soul, therefore, I am more covert about exposing my personality flaws than he is!

# WHAT THE HECK WAS THAT ABOUT?

There is a T.V. series called <u>Leverage</u>. In one segment, one of the actors is impersonating a pastor at a wedding. He makes the observation that while everyone seems to think that marriage is about candlelight dinners while gazing across the table into your beloved's eyes, in reality, marriage is like going to WalMart!

To me, that was a profound description of what marriage really is. I knew a woman who, having been married once and devastated by it, decided she didn't like being married. What she did like was the feeling of being in love; the rush of someone desiring her, taking her out to expensive dinners, showering her with outrageous gifts (no one ever did that for me!) and offering to mow her lawn without her even asking (I could get used to that!)

She disliked the planning and preparing of meals part, the part about the husband sitting in front of the T.V. and ignoring her, and the picking up dirty clothes and washing them part of a marriage. So, she decided to have the best of both worlds and date someone until the thrill, the newness wore off and then end the relationship.

Unfortunately, these supposedly superficial relationships took a toll on her though; because she became attached to some degree to every individual she dated. Since her purpose was to "enjoy being in love", she fell in love with every individual she dated. I tell you, she was stalked more than any person I've ever met…and I worked for a Victim Services Unit in a major Police Department for five years.

This woman tore herself apart literally going from one "drama" to another, always secretly hoping for a marriage proposal which, unsurprisingly, never came. After all, she had set her intentions on having fun and not getting too deeply involved with another. You can't really get married and refrain from getting too deeply involved. She called to herself what she wanted, yet, when she got it, she didn't want it anymore. I've since lost track of her but I do know that she was an extremely lonely individual who always kept others at arms length but who deeply longed for close human contact and friendship.

Once, when we were walking along a frozen stream, she started silently crying. She said the stream reminded her of her life; that she was vital and alive under the ice but she just couldn't seem to break through the frozen part of her life! Later, in our friendship, she said that she had gotten too close to me and that it wasn't safe to get too close to others.

This gorgeous, vital, intelligent, woman was falling back on her life's experiences…it wasn't safe to get too close to another human being, they can't be trusted! The things we do to one another. <u>Please</u> think before causing pain to another human being!!!

While she tried to protect herself from being hurt by not taking any risks, or opening her heart, she created great pain in her life and closed the door to attaining fulfillment.

Marriage is just like going to WalMart. It's not all glitz and glitter, that's for sure.

As a kid, I always wanted to have a "bestest" friend (although I never could because I wasn't allowed out of the house except to go to school, pay the bills and purchase groceries), in whom I could confide, someone who wouldn't judge me but who would understand or at least listen to me.

That's what marriage or a partnership is all about…two individuals coming together for a mutual purpose because they genuinely care for each other. It's just like being able to live with your "bestest" friend, it's having someone to watch your back, it's having someone to shore you up, to encourage you when you're down or doubt yourself (they never doubt you—well?), someone to support you and having someone to share what's going on in your life even if it is just that the washing machine broke again! Everything is so much more tolerable when you can share the burden and know that someone is on your side! To me, it's a feeling of belonging…which I have never experienced before…it's EVERYTHING! Understand that I am not promoting marriage – it's certainly not for everyone…only for the brave of heart - - - **THE <u>VERY</u> BRAVE OF HEART!**

Our society promotes autonomy but we are instinctively social animals. Numerous books have been written on the drawbacks of codependency---yet, we ARE codependent! Let's face it, how many of us can be totally self-sufficient? I'm talking totally…create your own energy source, provide all of your own food, make your own clothing, build your own shelter from scratch? Have any of your friends ever built an automobile? We need others to survive…there is strength in numbers.

Yes, there are survivalists who do just that …they "survive", they can exist on their own and I feel certain that there are many of us who also could survive on our own if it was necessary, but it's not! Not yet, anyway! Living life is so much easier as well as more pleasurable when you have someone else you can count on and someone to share your life with. So don't jump ship if your ship isn't sinking, just because you've been told that it's unhealthy to be codependent and that you need to be autonomous! Having someone that you genuinely love and who genuinely loves you in return is one of <u>THE</u> most sacred gifts you can ever expect to receive! Cherish it!

# SPIRITUAL COMMUNICATION
# OR SELFISH BANTER

It's not that others resist your message, it's the delivery of the message that they often resist.

Have your every tried, unsuccessfully, having a heart to heart conversation about your relationship with a significant other? Gosh, here you are really trying to communicate; you pour your heart out, you bare your soul...what the hell else can you do to get your point across? Yet, your soul mate, your significant other, the person you love...once loved?, either rolls their eyes..clear to the back of their head, gets defensive (why in the heck would they get defensive, you're the injured party here), makes excuses, argues about the specifics or validity of your statements or flat out gets up and walks away!

Gosh! You've all heard the saying about catching more flies with honey than with a fly swatter? Therein lies the problem. No one is receptive to hearing about their own flaws, (because in their own muddled minds, they don't have any), how wrong they are or how often they've failed.

Although you are trying to communicate honestly and sincerely, (perhaps too honestly... we are all delicate flowers here who cannot tolerate too much of the truth...for it so offends us!), you must try to do it in a non-antagonistic way. No one is to blame here... you see things one way, they see them another. You are two individuals who simply have different points of view.

Consider how you would present your case to the Board of Directors, City Council, if you have to go to Court (I'm sorry), how do you plead your case? Do you accuse the other, berate them for causing you so much pain, try to make them suffer? I don't think so!

Just because you are genuinely trying to problem solve with your partner, lover, friend, does not mean that "tactfulness" goes out the window. What you are striving for here is for others to be receptive to what you are saying rather than having the hair on the back of their head standing straight up. Just put yourself in their place…how would you feel if you were on the receiving end of this "soul searching" conversation…perhaps a course in compassionate communication might be in order.

Here is an "automatic writing" about this very situation to illustrate the point. Spirit is so subtle sometimes! NOT!

My Dearest Spirit,

Did you just see what I did? I've already started…I'm standing up for myself and making my wishes known! Phil, for the second or third day in a row came upstairs when I was doing my writing, noticed I was writing and walked into the kitchen anyway and attempted to engage me in conversation.

Normally, I would have just ignored it but I have repeatedly asked him not to disturb or interrupt me when I meditate or write. He has continued to ignore my requests. He is such a sweet man and I don't want to be too hard on him but sometimes, he is just clueless! I feel it is very important both for our marriage, and for me personally, to raise his awareness and to assist him to be more thoughtful and considerate of the needs of others.

So, I went down to the basement when he went down and explained AGAIN that it is very important to me that I have my privacy both when I meditate and do my writing. I pointed out that this was the third day in a row that he has come up, noticed I was writing and tried to engage me in conversation. I explained very nicely, I think, that the next time he comes up and finds me writing or meditating, he needs to turn around and go back downstairs. He apologized and agreed to do that. Hopefully this training is not going to have to be an on-going experience with him. But hey—I've started!

Love,
Nancy

Nancy,

Yes you have and I was exceedingly proud of the fact that you maintained your composure and didn't turn it into a "tug of war". Most of the learning we do is learning to change our own behavior so that others want to accommodate us! You know the old saying, "you can catch more bees with honey".

Keep up the good work Nancy—your first day of training and you have already accomplished much!

*Spirit*

Geesh, talk about anti-climatic, that was a little disheartening. I expected so much more….well, praise for putting Phil in his place and standing up for myself, NOT a subtle chastisement or implication that I usually turn things into a "tug of war"! Why would I ever do that? What would it accomplish? Instead, I just ignore every slight and "stuff" my frustration…oops, until it eventually reaches volcanic proportions and then I blow! Okay, but I still think Spirit could have been a little more supportive, after all, I did bare my soul and confide my every thought! It just goes to show, that we all have our own perceptions of how things go down and my perception is that Spirit could have been a little gentler, kinder—perhaps even…taken my side?!

# THE WICKED STEPMOTHER…
## FACT OR FICTION?

Do you remember the first time you saw <u>Cinderella</u> or <u>Snow White</u>? Didn't your heart go out to the innocent child and didn't you just despise their wicked, evil, vile, stepmothers? You thought it was just a fairy tale---after all, rational, responsible, mature adults don't really act that way. Well….think again! Not that they are rational, responsible or mature and yet, they are considered to be adults—what is this world coming to?

In family therapy it is common knowledge that the so called "problem" member of the family is frequently in reality, the healthiest of all the other family members.

While the rest of the family remain unaware of the dysfunctional family dynamics that are going on, the so labeled "problem" member whether it be a child, parent, spouse or the family dog, is the only one who actually sees the situation for what it really is – dysfunctional! This "problem" individual then acts out in order to call attention to the real problem, that of dysfunctional family dynamics, while the rest of family blindly continues life in this unhealthy and sometimes dangerous manner. The other family members who subconsciously are working together to maintain the dysfunctional family dynamics are suddenly appalled when a member of their own family, usually the scapegoat, behaves so irrationally.

Kids are great at this. They know a lot more than adults in most instances, about what is actually occurring in the family. As a former Sunday School Teacher of three year olds…I guarantee, kids know <u>everything </u>that is happening in their family!

Women, not to pick on any genders here, frequently seem unable or unwilling to accept the off-spring of another woman, especially when it is the child of her husband's ex-wife. Isn't it a mystery that in nature, a wild, unsophisticated animal will adopt and care for an orphaned animal of another species, yet an intelligent, seemingly compassionate human being cannot even bring themselves to care for the offspring of their own species simply because the offspring belongs in part, to the ex-wife of their spouse?

Perhaps it is because this child was in his/her mother's womb for nine months, more or less, and bonded with the mother, or perhaps it is because the child displays physical similarities to their mother. For whatever reason, men seem more able to accept their wives children from a previous marriage than do women.

If you hate or resent the mother of the child, then you are absolutely going to hate or resent the child, for after all, the child is a product of the mother. You want your own flesh and blood child to receive all the attention, all the privileges and you certainly don't want to share those privileges with some "half breed"!

Ladies, come on…this is a child, a living human being. This poor kid did not sin against you nor did this child hurt you or your spouse. Come on…you're the adult here…GROW UP!

And men, ha, you actually thought you were going to get away scott free didn't you? It was not meant to be. Where are the fathers of these emotionally and many times physically abused kids? Can't they hear? Don't they see? Have you ever heard the term, Guilt by Association? If you happen to be with someone when they rob a bank – guess what? You don't get to pass go; instead you get to go to prison too! You can't claim "ignorance"!

Did not you ever hear the phrase, "Do unto others as ye would have others do unto you"? Well, guess what slick, that phrase applies to <u>your</u> <u>children</u> as well!

# ATTACK OF THE KILLER GRAPE

Gosh, remember all the talk about "wake up" calls and that your soul is trying desperately to get your attention? Remember me saying that the choice is yours (Oh good Lord – do I really HAVE to do this?), that you can do it the easy way or you can do it the hard way?

Well, here's the thing…perhaps, I was starting to get just a little pious. I am, after all, writing a book about self knowledge and personal growth. One would think (that's what you get for thinking) that I, therefore, by all rights, should have attained self knowledge and personal growth. You might imagine that I have explored every cavern and crevice on the pathway to my soul. You could also just as easily imagine that I'm full of (?) it!

To continue…on my way to a "spiritual" panel discussion, I stopped at an organic, natural market to pick up some "good for you, junk food", you know; almonds, rice crackers and of course, a bottle of Greek, organic, extra Virgin, cold pressed olive oil.

I walked through the front door, made my way back to the restrooms (by now you've probably figured out that restrooms play a major part of my life) and was walking back from the restrooms, past the deli when suddenly, out of nowhere, I was attacked by a killer grape! My right foot slipped on the little monster and went right out from under me… O U C H! Double O U C H! The hell with it….Triple O U C H!

It all happened so quickly; my knee was suddenly engulfed by sharp, pulsating pain…I was feeling nauseated and I started to hyperventilate! As I tried in vain to sit up, my eyes found my left knee. Even through my jeans (designer jeans, by the way) I could see that my knee was seriously injured…my first clue here being that I saw a bone protruding against the material of my jeans (<u>designer jeans</u>)!

Some guy was standing there saying that he saw the whole thing and that there was "grease" on the floor; that he had never seen anything so bad before. To accelerate my panic even more, a lady, taking notes who worked at the store, commented that she also had never seen such a severe injury …here I am listening to all of this and trying desperately not to continue hyperventilating and pass out!

The paramedics were called, and I and my <u>one and only</u> pair of designer jeans were whisked off in an ambulance, not before by the way, they actually cut the left pants leg off of my designer jeans; (sob) to the nearest hospital! I've had those jeans for seven years…I seldom ever wear them because I didn't want them to get worn out!

In the ER it was discovered that my left knee, along with my life for at least the next ten months, had exploded upon hitting the hard surface of the floor thereby causing my patella tendon to tear in half by approximately 27 centimeters.

I was soooo bummed! Here I was, little miss self-actualization, who had just embarked on a new career, I was writing a book! For Pete's sakes is there no respect in this world? My entire life was suddenly turned upside down and I, for one, did not like it.

This "little incident", as the insurance agent for the organic, natural, holistic, food market referred to it, caused me considerable pause. Why on earth did this happen to me, of all people…I'm a good person, I help <u>everyone!</u> What lesson was I supposed to learn from this? You mean other than the fact that a store with customers walking in all the time should be responsible enough to keep their floors clean? Seriously, there wasn't even a

"Caution – Wet Floor" sign, or better yet, "Caution – Killer Grapes lurking behind every isle"! Come on, that's just not fair!

I was getting no answers, just more and more frustrated! Finally, in desperation, I begrudgingly sat down and wrote an automatic writing letter to Spirit. It follows:

Dearest Spirit,

All knowing and all loving Spirit, please reveal to me the purpose of my accident. If it serves no purpose what did I do to cause this to happen?

Thank you.

Nancy, the Answer Seeker

(Perhaps, I sometimes take myself a little too seriously? but hey, I had just shattered my knee!)

Nancy,

The reason this happened is to get you to slow down and attend to <u>your</u> life both spiritual and physical. You seem to think you can right all the wrongs of the world and the behavior of others when all you have to work with is yourself!

You need to turn your attention inward: what is best for you, what do you desire, what do you crave, yearn for, wish for above all else?

What is it you truly seek? It is all yours Nancy, now is the time to reach out and take it! Phil can provide for himself, Tim no longer needs you, your children are grown. What you have here is you. What will you do with you?

*Spirit*

Which is why I told you (here, take my advice, I'm not using it) that only you had all the information you needed to live a good life.

Some well meaning individual might tell you that the Universe is against you (come on!), that you need to go to confession to seek absolution for your <u>many</u> sins or that for only 30 sessions at the low, low cost of $200.00 per session from your friendly Tarot reader, your life will turn around for the better. Well, my dear friend, no matter how friendly or well-intentioned the advice, it just won't "take" until YOU seek out and find your own solution.

Not everyone, hopefully no one else,, is going to have to encounter a "killer grape" in order to finally listen to their soul desperately trying to communicate with them. The really sad thing is that the more you ignore your soul, your intuition, the quieter it gets until you can barely hear it and then it may finally quit talking to you all together! After all, no one likes to be ignored or minimized, much less your all wise soul! Seconds before my accident, I heard a voice in my head saying, "You need to slow down!" Well, I'm definitely slowed now!

For the very first time in my life I am "allowing" another human being to take care of my needs, (Hell, I can't even go to the bathroom by myself!)…my husband, you remember him, "Mr. Maddening, I'm Day, He's Night", oh, how embarrassing!

For all intensive purposes, the lower part of my leg is separated from the top portion and it just dangles! I have to physically lift it to sit down as it has to be kept immobilized and straight. My darling husband (oh, how quickly our tone changes) has to physically hold the bottom part of my leg and lower it onto a footrest every time I sit down and hold it and raise it each and every time I get up from a sitting position; when I go to bed (and remember, we've already discussed how many potty breaks I require).

So, BEWARE, lest you think you are superior in any way to someone else, for that very same inferior human being may very well be the only one who is willing to assist you to the restroom! Oh Gosh, you have NO idea how very much I am <u>hating</u> committing this to writing!

# "THE MORNING AFTER"

Well, surgery was yesterday morning. My God/Goddess, I did not know I was capable of experiencing so much pain!

First of all, they came in and gave me some sort of a block to help alleviate any pain during surgery – HUH? I was going to be unconscious during the surgery; usually you don't feel anything once they put you out. This, of course involved giving me a shot that just stung a little, just like a large and very upset bee sting, directly into my groin. The purpose of this shot was, of course to alleviate the pain of receiving the block! Then came, the much talked about block…again right into my groin. This little procedure felt very much as though someone had acquisitioned my very powerful Bosch drill and was proceeding to drill a large stake directly into my groin! Was I hallucinating? Had I misunderstood? Here I thought the shot was to prevent me from experiencing horrific pain when the block was administered! Someone had not been totally upfront here!

When I awoke from the anesthesia the surgeon had a little surprise for me. Oh goody! Instead of one, I had received two surgical steel plates in my knee, more is better, right? At that point, I didn't even care, I just wanted to get the heck out of that place and go home to be with my family which consists of two Doberman and five cats…oh yeah, I have a husband too!

In spite of the accident and the pain incurred, I really have to say that I am counting my blessings. Everything really worked out and everyone was so kind and accommodating. This type of behavior is something I am definitely not accustomed to, I must say.

The day of the accident, I was whisked to the emergency room of the closest hospital. One of the nurses commented that she had been working in the ER for over five years and had never seen such a severe break. The second nurse, who had also been an ER nurse for over five years agreed. So, you can imagine my dismay when the on-call surgeon said he had to do surgery the next morning and that I would have to spend the night in the hospital.

I didn't know this guy; what were his credentials? Was he an ambulance chaser? Besides, I couldn't stay the night, I had to go home and get my five cats inside the house before some hungry coyote or raptor decided to have a late night snack! I let the kids out during the day, after first making sure there are no predators around and then bring them "willingly", (no kidding) in before dark. So, at 10:00 p.m., I was released from the hospital.

Early the next morning I called my primary physician to tell her what happened and get a referral from her. She gave me a referral and I called the office explaining that I had shattered my knee and my patella tendon had split in half separating by 27 centimeters and that I had to have surgery within fourteen days. I was told that the surgeon could not possibly perform surgery on me because his schedule was full for the next two months! However, I was told that if I wanted to schedule an office visit, he could possibly refer me to someone else. What the heck, I'm not used to frequenting with orthopedic surgeons and therefore did not know any by reputation.

When I went in, much to my surprise, the surgeon, after reviewing my file and looking forward to the "challenge", said he could perform surgery on my knee the following Monday, apologizing that I would have to wait six days in agony before going in for surgery. He originally had squeezed me in for surgery at night from 7:30 p.m. until 12:30 a.m. and I would have to spend the night! This was not to be an arthroscopic surgery; I was playing with the big boys now. I would have to have an 8 inch incision in order to reconstruct the sawdust which was now my knee cap and put in a metal plate!

I asked if there were any way I could go home that evening explaining about my animals and was told that he does not do the scheduling and I would have to call his scheduler the next morning to see if they could help me out. Well…first thing the next morning, guess what?, his office called ME to say they had rescheduled me for first thing on Monday morning, from 7:00 a.m. until 12:30 p.m. and…I would get to go home that same afternoon!

My friends, family and neighbors have all been absolutely great! Everyone brought over food (my husband was in heaven) and a few of my neighbors even came over and cleaned for me…believe me that must've been quite a sacrifice because after two weeks with all my animals and husband, my house was more than a little dirty! People sent prayers and healing energy, I was on more prayer chains and received more Reiki than I ever thought possible!

This experience has really taught me about the basic goodness of others. I've really never expected much from other people because usually I've been the care giver and they are the recipients. Also, my childhood taught me that others could definitely not be relied upon and were never to be trusted.

An example from my adolescence will help you to understand why: One day when I was a freshman in high school a classmate came over to borrow a homework paper. She had been ill, l always made straight A's (intuitively knowing that this was my only key to escape from my happy little family), so it made sense that she would come over to borrow my A+ homework paper. This rationale however, seemed to elude my father who immediately became enraged (by now you've probably figured out that becoming enraged was this guy's coping style of choice!) the instant she was out the door. He turned beet red, starting pacing and yelling that she was a whore! He wanted to know why the hell a whore was coming to our house to see me…honestly; I think he was just jealous that she hadn't come to see him!

Alas, unfortunately for me, my mouth has always had a life of it's own! Seriously!!! My instinctive, rather than life preserving response was, "Well dad, if anyone knows who all the whores in town are, it would certainly be you!" You can just imagine how well received that little observation was, astute as it may have been. Apparently, having run out of anything else to say, my father shut his fist and punched me right in the face! As previously stated….behavior speaks volumes therefore, I surmised that he was really angry! Then, much to my delight, he told me that he was sick of me and ordered me to get the hell out of his house. I didn't wait around for a second invitation. I wasted no time running (I didn't even put on my shoes) out the back door and into the alley. No sooner had I reached the alley when out of the corner of my eye, I caught a glimpse of his car. Couldn't this guy make up his mind? I literally jumped into one of those large, concrete dumpsters, cutting my foot on a piece of broken glass, while attempting to avoid yet another family reunion. To this day, I am not big on family reunions.

As soon as his car passed, I ran to my principal's apartment and knocked on the door only to be told by his wife, presumably, that he was not home. Being the tenacious kid (with a big mouth – sigh, a <u>very</u> big mouth) that I was, I then ran to my guidance counselor's home, still shoeless! She informed me that we had to go to the police station because my dad was going to report me as a run away. I tried in vain, to talk her out of it, explaining that he had told me to leave and that I had his permission, but no one ever listens to kids, especially of the big mouth variety!

Somehow my guidance counselor had been able to get a hold of my principal because he was waiting for us when we arrived at the Rocky Ford Police Station. After hearing my account of the events of the day and listening to what my guidance counselor and principal described as a sweet, smart, little girl who was always showing up to school with black eyes, swollen lips and bruises, the Chief of Police dispatched a young officer to go retrieve dad, saying that he could probably be found at one of the two local bars. Good guess as the officer brought dad right in.

It was a really weird experience; I didn't immediately recognize my own father! He was smiling and joking, and seemed to be cooperative. Of course, he denied any abuse whatsoever saying that I had been a problem since birth and was very self destructive, implying…no implication here…he was blatantly stating that all the bruises, black eyes etc., were self inflicted. That's my Dad…for better or for worse!

And then it happened, the Chief of Police ordered the young officer to drive dad and me back home! How could this be happening? Hadn't he heard what everyone said? Oh my God, I was being sent home to be executed! Terrified, I begged the Chief not to make me go back home. I told him that my father hated me and that I hated him and that dad wanted me dead! I implored him to send me to reform school instead but as previously stated, sometimes no one will listen to kids.

Then, there I was sitting in the backseat (no less) of the police car while dad and the officer sat up front. I couldn't believe this was really happening…by nightfall I would be dead! In a sad, perhaps masochistic way, I was even wondering how dad was going to kill me. Would he just beat me to death, or would he try to make it look like an "accident", perhaps tie me up, place me on the street and repeatedly run over me?

When I was younger I had prayed and prayed for God to please let me die and now that my request was being granted…I wanted to live! Guess it goes to show that we're never satisfied; you get what you want and you don't want it anymore. But somehow, these thoughts didn't seem to make my predicament any less tragic.

And then…A MIRACLE HAPPENED! The young officer, who looked way too young to even be in possession of a driver's license turned to my jovial father and in that moment, pardoned my death sentence and literally saved my life! He told dad that they (the officers) were going to be "checking on his daughter" to make sure that I was okay. The officer stated that while they couldn't go to our home, they would go to school and to church or check on me when I was walking home from school. The officer then proceeded to say that if they found one bruise, or cut, much less a black eye, they would hunt dad down, lock him in jail and throw away the key!

My father protested indignantly and very loudly that he had never and would never harm his own daughter. He stated that I was a liar and he feared that I was on drugs. The young officer, now also raising his voice, proclaimed that I was a sweet, little girl, a straight A student, that all of my teachers adored me while dad was nothing but a F_ _ _ _ _ drunk and that he (dad) just better hope that I didn't "accidently" trip and fall or anything else to harm myself because if I did dad's drinking and whoring days would come to an end forever!

Whew! That must've really scared dad because the next morning I heard him talking to mom. He was telling her how very much he hated me and that he wanted nothing more than to see me dead but that the cop was right, it wasn't worth spending the rest of his life in jail just to kill me! And from that day forth, the beatings stopped!

I was never beaten again; I was not even, ever again pushed or slapped! See, you can pray for something get it and then change your mind and pray for something else and get it too!

# FAMILY DYNAMICS

Most parents don't deliberately induce this much devastation on their children but beware of the Blind leading the Blind!

Most adults, unfortunately, are controlled by pain and/or fear. It seems astonishing that someone who suffered as a child would knowingly inflict pain on their own children. Or would they? Knowingly that is? We are all programmed from early childhood to "do the right thing" as written in the chapter under Parental Responsibilities in the Bible; (???) such as respect your elders; (even if they have never done anything to earn *anyones* respect), share your toys; only to get punished for not taking care of your toys when someone with whom you have shared the damn toy smashes it into a million pieces (it's a wonder there aren't more children in psyche wards), children should be seen and not heard; big boys don't cry and don't express emotion; (that way little boys can grow up to be cold, heartless, control freaks just like their daddy), don't talk back; even if some adult is blatantly wrong and on an ego trip or a bully taking advantage of a little kid. There is so little time to enforce the many rules on our young but someone's gotta do it to protect (oops, I meant "subject") our little ones to inherit the unhappy, rule-laden, fulfillment deprived and dreadful lives that we ourselves are now experiencing.

Have you ever observed a very small child being admonished for not keeping up? The little tyke is taking at least ten steps for every one that his five foot eleven mother and six foot four father are taking. Yet, kids need to learn at an early age to obey their parents. If it really is that crucial to get to Starbucks in record breaking time, wouldn't you think one of these mental giants could figure out that it would be easier just to pick up the little guy and carry him there?

Oh no, it is so much more fun to show the kid "who's the boss" and to strengthen those vocal cords. Unfortunately, the brain is seldom engaged under "chest pounding" circumstances.

A child is filled with awe, wonderment and pleasure upon entering into this magnificent world. There are so many things to see, to do, and to experience. Our world is filled with marvelous creatures; butterflies and birds that soar above our heads; "how come we can't fly mommy?" Rolly pollys curl up into perfect balls…"can you do that Daddy"? There are flowers to smell and to pick to give to mommy, rabbits, skunks…did I say skunks? Oops, typo, ---no typo, skunks are also God's creatures and as such are worthy of respect… DEEP respect! Remember that ALL creatures, yes that includes you and your child of the Divine, have a purpose…even those little groundhogs that your daddy loves to shoot and kill just for the sport of it Johnny.

Simply because most adults, in all fairness, because they are trying desperately to earn a living, to provide for their families and because it is correct and proper and macho not to smile, have forgotten how to enjoy the wonders of Nature, they then try to prevent their children from stopping to smell the flowers on a hike, (after all, they have to hurry and finish the hike so that they can then hurry and get back home to plan their next family outing). The little guy can't stop to catch a worm, (ugh, it's unsanitary) to present as a treasured gift to his cherished parents. Pretty soon, kids grow up with inferiority complexes, everything they do is wrong, no matter how hard they try, they just can't seem to please their "perfect" parents. They don't seem to fit in, they don't get good enough grades, they're not athletic enough, they don't want to play football like daddy…they want to play with their butterfly collection instead.

There is a song, I think by Jim Croce, I don't know the title but it saddens me every time I hear it. The story is that the dad was always too busy to play catch with his little son, or to spend much time with the kid at all. The little boy who worshipped his father always said, "when I grow up I'm going to be just like you dad" and he did. When the father was old and lonely, he would call his son who was too busy with his own family and business to give his aging father any of his time. The father then sings, "he grew up to be just like me, my son grew up to be just like me." Why is it that the human being who is so much more intelligent supposedly, than any other species, seldom seems to figure things out until it is too late?

Just because the needs of your soul were ignored as a youngster, because you were indoctrinated with rules, because others imposed what they wanted for you instead of what you really needed, because you were inundated by the beliefs and emotions of others, because you have become a spiritual amnesiac and experience no joy in your life … is that any reason to impose the very same life sentence on your own child who looks to you for guidance, for protection, for wisdom,…for LOVE?

These are precious little souls and you have been entrusted with the highest purpose imaginable, that of helping and teaching them to grow, to flourish into the individual that their souls chose for them to be. You were never intended to control them or to make them into miniature robots of yourself!

I am not advocating that you refrain from guiding or disciplining your children when needed but what I am suggesting is that whatever you do, do it in love—not to "wipe the smile off anyone's face"! And do what you, as a parent believe in your heart is for the highest good and growth of your child—rather than to show them who is the boss, or who is in control. Life is the most valuable possession we have and you have been charged with just such a human life..this is a sacred responsibility. PLEASE, take it seriously!

# SISTER SANDPAPER OR, ... THE TRIPLETS

My ex-husband and I were, for several years, Elders in a Bible packing, Full Gospel, Dancing in the Spirit, Speaking in Tongues, Non-Denominational "Whew", church. Well, that's not quite true, my husband was an Elder, as women were submissive and subject to the rule of their husbands and could never advance in the church unless their "cover" or husband advanced.

In other words, the women did ALL the work and the men took all the glory. It was much like childbirth; the women carry the child for approximately nine months, then deliver, usually in excruciating pain and then the proud "papa" exclaims, "my boys can swim", the guys all smoke a cigar and the little woman is left to get her vagina stitched up! Now, modern couples in order to get the father more invested in the birth of his own child, proclaim that "WE are pregnant", "WE are getting ready to deliver". WOW, have WE been prepped yet, are WE dilated, are WE getting a spinal? Do WE think we're going to die yet if WE have one more contraction? Anyway, being a member of this church was very much like childbirth, if you were a women. It was GREAT for the men.

I was once the recipient of a very potent and accurate teaching from our pastor's "wife", no less. Of course, the class was comprised of all women, as she was not fit to deliver a message to MEN! Only GOD, or an individual of equal stature, such as a male could do that! The "jist" of the message was that if you encounter a person who is particularly difficult to get along with, who rubs you the wrong way or someone you just cannot stand and you want off the face of the earth NOW either in your neighborhood, school, or place of employment, (certainly there are no such "persons" in our churches) and, of course, said person is referred to as "Sister" Sandpaper, for obvious reasons…duh, a "Brother" Sandpaper is unheard of…at least on our planet!

Back to the point Nancy: If, you are working yourself up to a frenzy trying to escape, destroy or discredit "her" or, if you are at the point of moving from your neighborhood, changing schools or jobs to avoid "her", then perhaps you should reconsider. What is it that you need to learn from all of this? What you see in others is a reflection of what is within you. If you do not learn, grow and change from this experience with the "she" Devil, unfortunately, the very next neighborhood, school or business you become involved in will, rest assured, have not only one, but two or even three (depending on how self-deluded you are) Sister Sandpapers!

We are presented with less than perfect (in contrast to ourselves, of course), individuals in an effort to teach us soul lessons and to accelerate our soul growth….you'd think, however, that God/Goddess/Spirit could come up with a better, easier and less painful plan. Regrettably, my plan to annihilate the jerks, may not have as long lasting or life altering effects…but it would initially feel SO MUCH BETTER!

Until we mature spiritually and accept others for who they are and acknowledge that we are all on different paths, and what is "right" for one is not necessarily "right" for the other…we will continue to encounter the same type of individual who "pushes our DAMN buttons, ON PURPOSE, premeditated and with malice!!!" Sigh!

As an example, I am allergic to penicillin; penicillin saves lives but for me, it could very well end my life! We are all different, unique individuals with our own agendas, idiosyncrasies and paths to follow. There is NOT one prescribed path for ALL!

Diversity is the key! We learn, we accept and we grow! We all love diversity, until we don't, and then,… we just destroy it. We kill the Satan worshipper, or worse, we just let them bleed out and hang on that cross indefinitely! Serves them right for daring to be different and...who in the heck do they think they are anyway thinking that THEY have the answers? Especially, if their answers don't coincide <u>exactly</u> with ours!

In my "humble" opinion, not wanting to be crucified, (I hate blood, especially my own!), I firmly believe that IF Jesus were to return to this earth, although he's probably too smart for that, we would hang him again! It would serve him right for making the same mistake twice, right? Gosh, we are such <u>S L O W</u> learners! WHY are we so threatened by what is not familiar to us or <u>exactly like us?</u> Open mindedness apparently is no longer necessary for survival...or is it and we just haven't figured it out yet. Oh well, we all make mistakes...it was just ONE life! And, he was <u>just</u> the son of a carpenter...not like he was the CEO of a major corporation or anything!

What has happened to the concept of new frontiers, of exploration, of learning from others? Do we ALL have to be clones or robots to peacefully co-exist? And what happened to..."We are ALL created equal"? Did God/Goddess make some sort of horrible mistake and it is up to us to rectify it? No wonder the second coming is taking so long...if I were God, I'd be stalling too!

The thing is...we are very much like athletes training for the Olympics! We practice, we practice more and then...we practice more and then...we practice more until we can perfect our skills in whatever sport we are competing in.

Why should life be any different? Just like an athlete, we are given ample opportunities to perfect our social and spiritual skills until we no longer "need" or are dependent on the acceptance or validation of others because we now KNOW that we have both from the Divine source. We no longer have to prove anything to anybody because WE ROCK!!!

I think it was in a Shakespearian play that the verse "me thinks ye protest too much" came about. When you know you're good, you're good. Kinda like, no ones going to call a 6'7", 305 lb. lineman a wimp! And you know, said lineman doesn't go around trying to convince others that he's not a wimp either...wonder why that is?

In retrospect, it is absolutely frightening how much we ignore our own "radar" warnings, which is our own soul trying to speak to us and instead listen to what others think we should do or should not do in our lives, just so that we can receive the validation and acceptance of another! We literally place ourselves in harm's way just so that we can gain acceptance of another or not hurt the feelings of another individual who thinks they know more about what is better for us than we do or, ...who feels that their needs override our needs and our values.

Years ago, my ex and I were skiing with another couple (Elders in our Bible packing, dancing in the spirit, full-gospel, non denominational, speaking in tongues church). It was towards the end of the day, we were all very tired, the slopes were icy, and visibility was poor. My friend suggested that we let the guys go up on one more run and that she and I go get a cup of hot chocolate. Yum, it sounded like a great idea to me. However, when I mentioned our plan to my then husband, he stated that we had spend a fortune on ski tickets and he thought in order to get the "most bang for our buck" we both needed to go up on one more run and then we could both meet our friends for hot chocolate later.

Although I was so tired my legs were literally shaking, "the good, little wife" went back up for one last run. Little did I know that it literally was going to be the last run of the season for me. As we reached the top, a mist descended upon the entire mountain covering it with an eerie fog thus decreasing visibility even more. I started down the slope with visions of a warm fire and hot chocolate dancing in my head. Even though I was a fairly accomplished skier and knew better, when I hit a patch of black ice, I locked my knees!

If you would've been there, and lucky for you that you weren't that day, you would've thought I was training for the Olympics. I executed the most amazing full flip in the air, well except for one little thing...I landed on my face! The thought ran through my mind that this was too much pain for me to handle and I blacked out temporarily, only to come to while sliding down the mountain on my face directly toward a little boy around seven or eight years of age who had fallen and was sitting on the ground crying.

I desperately dug my ski's and fingers into the snow trying to avoid hitting the little guy as he would've been thrown over the edge of the mountain had I hit him. I finally stopped within a foot of a very terrified little boy, who took one look at my face, quit crying, got to his feet and skied off hollering for help! No wonder, when I later looked in the mirror, even I would have gone hollering down the mountain, if I could've skied, that is. When my husband found me, I remember telling him that I thought I had "broke my whole face"! My right eye was bulging out of my head and was black and blue; just like the mountain, we had been on a blue-black slope, I like to color coordinate! My entire face was swollen to about three times bigger than it normally is and was covered with rug burn type rash. No wonder the little boy was so frightened; I looked very much like a monster!

Not wanting to be put into one of those "body bags" utilized by the ski patrol, I attempted to ski but mostly slid on my butt the entire way down the slope to the clinic. Alas, this is not the climax of my story- - -THERE'S MORE! And there always is, isn't there? When you don't listen to your own inner guidance.

The very next year, yup, I didn't even skip a year to repeat the same mistake. My husband and I were skiing on the very same blue-black slope with the very same friends from our very same Bible-packing, (you get the jist) church. Once again towards the end of the day, my friend suggested that we girls stop and get a cup of hot chocolate. Now wouldn't you think that a fairly intelligent woman who had almost broken her neck just the year before on this same slope, under the same circumstances, with the same friends from the same church would listen to her intuition and get the heck off that slope? Well, if you did think that, you're wrong. Some people just don't learn from their mistakes! As they say, everything happens for a reason and if you can't serve as a good example….well, then, you can always serve as a BAD one; and I feel confident that my shortcomings will serve as a warning to someone out there!

When I told my husband that I was quitting for the day, it was like Déjà Vue. I swear it was like a recording of an old movie, even his words were an exact duplicate of what he had said the year before and all this time my inner guidance was literally screaming at me not to go up one more time. I didn't listen and that last run turned out to be the last run of my entire life! I fell on the <u>exact same spot</u> I had fallen the year previously but without the dramatic full flip—I kinda just flopped. Each time I tried to stand up my right knee would slip out of the socket and I would go down again. So that year's grand finale was me being taken off the mountain in the much dreaded Body Bag! Sometimes when you don't listen to your own soul, you literally end up in a Body Bag!

In both instances, I blatantly ignored my inner guidance system simply because I didn't want to upset someone else; I didn't want to endure the confrontation that would have ensued had I stood my ground nor did I want to be humiliated in front of our friends by getting into an argument in front of them. So, instead, I spend the next three to four months in a cast, totally dependent upon others to drive me to get groceries, to doctor's appointments (there were a lot of those) and anywhere else I needed to go. It was a very clear lesson in an ironic way: When you elect not to listen to yourself or take care of your own needs first – then you get to be dependent on others, not only for your transportation but for your welfare as well!

The obvious unspoken communication here is that we don't care about or trust ourselves as much as we do others. Why? Because we don't seem to think we can survive without the approval of others and so we do "whatever it takes" to win their approval. We tell our children not to give in to Peer Pressure, sadly we, as adults, should be following our own advice!

# CLUELESS IN NEW HAMPSHIRE

When my current husband (eeks, that sounds really weird, like I collect husbands or something), asked me to marry him, he stated that I could select three locations (yes, the same infuriating husband who helped me lift my leg to get in and out of bed…I'm Day and he's Night!) anywhere for our wedding and that he would then pick one out of the three locations I had selected and that is where we would be married! WOW! It was too good to be true! No, literally, it was TOO GOOD TO BE TRUE!

I selected Hawaii, somewhere in the mountains of Colorado and Las Vegas (we know a great Elvis impersonator and I thought it might be fun to get married in a little chapel with Elvis singing Love Me Tender). It was to be a special, very romantic, wedding, just him and me, even though my family and his family wanted to participate, we had decided (or so I thought) that it was the two of us who were going to be together for the rest of our lives (now I'm not so sure) and that we wanted to be alone, together, for this most sacred ceremony!

Guess again, my dear husband to be or, …not to be, decided all on his own, that we should get married back east in New Hampshire (had I mistakenly written down New Hampshire instead of Hawaii?) because every year on the Fourth of July, his family has a family reunion in New Hampshire at a lovely campsite. All his nieces and nephews and of course his mother and father, two brothers and sister and several of his friends were going to be there. He deduced that this made total sense: instead of his family having to travel someplace else since his parents live back east, and since they were getting on in age, and the entire family would be there anyway, that that's where we were going to be married. And, he had already told his entire family that we would be married in New Hampshire and they were all expecting us. Call me menopausal, I somehow felt betrayed, lied to, cheated (out of my own wedding) and certainly very distrustful of this man who was going to be my husband. What a dilemma!

What do most of us do when faced with a lose, lose situation? We decide that we are being unreasonable and that we should just grow up and think of someone else besides ourselves. I rationalized that, after all, I had been married before and this was Phil's first marriage (and now I understand fully why!) So, in spite of the fact, that we had <u>both</u> decided our wedding would be a quiet, romantic, little twosome; in spite of the fact that my six and a half year old grandson wanted very much to "give me away", in spite of the fact that my five year old granddaughter wanted to be the flower girl, and in spite of the fact that my daughter-in-law was pregnant and could not "fly" anywhere, I rationalized that this man was the love of my life and acquiesced to be married in New Hampshire.

WHY do <u>we do these things to ourselves?</u> No one holds a gun to our head and forces us to do anything yet, we allow others to lie, cheat and steal from us all in the name of keeping the peace or worse yet; in the name of Love! If it were truly Love, wouldn't it be reciprocal? Or, perhaps, it's because we don't think we, in ourselves are enough, and no one will like us or value us unless we are constantly sacrificing…our time, our ideas, our values. Yes, and even sometimes our very lives.

**The following poem by Nadine Stair has really touched my soul:**

## <u>IF</u> I HAD MY LIFE TO LIVE OVER

"I'd dare to make more mistakes next time. I'd relax, I would limber up. I would be sillier than I have been this trip. I would take fewer things seriously. I would take more chances. I would climb more mountains and swim more rivers. I would eat more ice cream and less beans. I would perhaps, have more actual troubles, but I'd have fewer imaginary ones!

You see, I'm one of those people who live sensibly and sanely hour after hour, day after day. Oh, I've had my moments, and if I had it to do over again, I'd have more of them. In fact, I'd try to have nothing else. Just moments, one after another, instead of living so many years ahead of each day. I've been one of those persons who never goes anywhere without a thermometer, a hot water bottle, a raincoat and a parachute. If I had to do it again, I would travel lighter than I have.

If I had my life to live over, I would start barefoot earlier in the spring and stay that way later in the fall. I would ride more Merry-Go-Rounds. I would pick more Daisies."

This is a daily reminder to me that we DO NOT have our lives to live over, at least not in this go round, so you might as well make the most out of each moment of every day. Once it's gone - - you can never have it back! You don't get "Do Overs" with your life!

You truly have been given The Keys to The Kingdom – YOU ARE WORTHY or they wouldn't have been given to you! Take them in gratitude and open the door...your door to a happy, prosperous, fulfilling life. God, Spirit, The Divine <u>wants</u> you to be happy; you want to be happy. So what's holding you back? YOU – it's all in your hands. If God be for you; who can be against you? No one; unless...you, are against yourself. Perhaps you don't think you really deserve happiness? Because...you're a sinner, or, you're unworthy. None of this is true. You deserve the very best because God wants to give it to you and, --and please... let's not go down that road of questioning God again! <u>No</u>!

You don't have to move mountains, you don't have to save the world- -your job is to have the best life you can possibly have and everything else will follow.

Here's a little secret (actually not so little) that I learned when I did an Automatic Writing on October 27, of 2013. I'm sharing this with you because it has changed the course of my life and I pray that it will have the same impact on yours:

"My Dearest Friend and Mentor,

Tell me what you are trying to teach me.

I <u>love</u> you,
Nancy"

"My Prize Student,

Actually you got it…the mystery of life is to simply live it Nancy. All else is frosting on the cake.

You will serve millions, you will reach into the hearts and souls of the multitudes, but if you do not live your life fully and wholly – every minute of it Nancy – all is lost. At least for you. For you must learn and know without any doubt that you are worthy and deserve to live your life <u>JUST FOR YOU!</u>

I love you,
*Spirit*"

Oh gosh, we scurry around like rats in a maze only to return to the exact, same location that we started at. We seem to be in such a hurry to go nowhere…we truly need to realize and appreciate WHO WE ARE and what we have NOW; quit worrying about the future or dwelling in the past - - <u>make the most of the present!</u> The rest will take care of itself!!!

I put this verse on the inside cover of all my handbooks for the many classes I teach:

# CHOICES

Your life is an unfolding journey. <u>You</u> are the creator of your experiences through your choice of perception, actions and reactions; your life directly reflects what you are currently believing, thinking and feeling.

## I CHOOSE:

**To live by choice, not by chance;**

**To make changes, not excuses,**

**To be motivated, not manipulated;**

**To be useful, not used;**

**To excel, not compete**

**I choose self esteem, not self pity,**

**I choose to listen to my inner voice, not the random opinion of others!**

Debbie Deaton

<u>PLEASE</u>, **choose to be happy! For by you being happy …you bring happiness into the world!**

**Namaste**